The Power of Self-belief

The Power of Self-belief

Oluseyi Eyitayo

JANUS PUBLISHING COMPANY
London, England

First published in Great Britain 2008
by Janus Publishing Company Ltd,
105-107 Gloucester Place,
London W1U 6BY

www.januspublishing.co.uk

British Library Cataloguing-in-Publication Data
A catalogue record for this book is available from the British Library

ISBN 978-1-85756-369-0

Cover Design: Warren Kujawski

Printed and bound in Great Britain

Contents

Chapter One

What are Beliefs?

To start with, let us agree that we can definitely disagree about what we assume to be belief. It certainly means different things to different people in all aspects. You might find it strange, how people tend to find it hard to give a simple but reasonable definition of what belief really is.

Despite this fact, most people spend most of their lives, if not all, believing in something they were brought up to believe as a child, as valid fact without ever trying to question why they believe what they believe.

There are a few factors responsible for our beliefs and, as you read, I would like you to pay close attention to the four main factors that are responsible for our beliefs, as mentioned in this chapter. What you will discover as you read, is how the definition and explanation of beliefs, can be described or defined in so many ways.

One thing you should be aware of is this: what one person defines belief to be, doesn't necessarily mean it's the final conclusion of what belief really is.

So What Really is Belief?

Some people describe belief to be the full assurance of something, in which one has full trust or confidence. The majority of people, when asked about what they understand belief to be, simply respond by saying, "I don't know, belief is the act of believing in something." Some would tell you that "belief" is to believe in what you were taught as a child by your parents, for example, religion.

In today's world we have thousands of religious groups, the most common of these including Christendom and Islam. If you were to study these faiths in comparison to each other, you may conclude that there is little significant difference between their core beliefs. There are, in fact, outstanding similarities between these two religious faiths, and their methods of worship. Furthermore, some of the similarities between Christians and Muslims include the fact that they both believe in and pray to a supreme being; referred to by Christians as "God", and by Muslims as "Allah".

Christians read from a holy book called the Bible, while the Muslims read from the book called the Koran. So far you have seen some of the similarities between the beliefs of the Christians and those of the Muslims. Let us take a look at some of their differences and some of the reasons for their beliefs.

Christians believe in a man having one wife, according to the doctrine of the "Holy Bible". Muslims believe a man has the right to marry more than one woman, as long as they are treated fairly. These are just a few comparisons between their religious beliefs.
I carried out a personal survey of two groups belonging to each of these religions, just to understand more about why they believed what they believed, and what they thought was responsible for it. According to my survey, most of their beliefs were based upon their upbringing by their parents. This

response came from a good 80% of both groups in total. The remaining 20% based it on other factors, such as personal life experiences and environment.

I personally was brought up in a Christian family and as a result I grew up as a Christian and followed the Christian doctrine, for example, reading the Bible, praying to God etc. Looking back now, I can confidently say my upbringing played an important role. As a Christian I was brought up to believe that, in order to get in touch with my spiritual being, I would have to get to know God.

At the age of twelve I experienced a change when I personally realized that not everyone shared the same beliefs as me especially religion-wise. This event aroused my curiosity, as it made me want to know why this was so. So I started a debate with my classmates specifically to understand why they didn't share the same view as me. I did a comparison between their view and mine, but still couldn't figure out clearly why there was a difference. Usually after our discussion I went home with a puzzled mind, trying to understand why my fellow classmates disagreed with my beliefs. This went on for a while, until I decided to ask my father why this was so. He explained to me that not everybody I met, or came across, would have the same beliefs as me, simply because of various factors, for example upbringing. Looking back now and judging from my father's statement and my own view of life in relation to my personal experiences, I would define belief to be undoubting faith in what we accept as right, true, or false. Bear in mind this is just from my point of view.

From my definition of what belief is, I now realize why I didn't quite understand why my classmates back then shared a different view to it. I believe this was simply due to the fact that I didn't understand the "why factor"; why they believed what they believed, the reasons behind it.

Having a belief, in today's society has some benefits, for example:

- Helps in enhancing positive thinking
- Provides a sense of direction
- Helps in developing faith.

Enhances Positive Thinking

Our beliefs certainly help in the enhancement of positive thinking because they simply create and build up courage, confidence etc., all of which are the necessary tools needed to achieve our goals, desires, or dreams.

Have you noticed how we tend to act when we feel passionately or deeply about something or someone, for example, a trusted friend, topic, or religion?

Our behaviour patterns usually change in response to what we believe, or how we feel. One of the common things we do is to try, as much as possible, to prove what we believe, for example in a discussion, by trying to bring it close, or relate it, to reality. You might wonder why we act this way, but don't be alarmed. It's simply because our subconscious mind has a lot to do with it. Still puzzled? This is how it works.

As a kid, whatever we have been brought up to believe in, gets stored in our subconscious minds, then making us act or behave in a certain manner. Our minds start to really develop at a very early stage, which is why we take in so much information especially our beliefs, for instance, our right from wrong etc. Most of this information can be retrieved at any time simply by a trigger. For example, let's imagine for a moment that you happen to see a phone which has been left on a bus on your way home. Some of the thoughts that would cross your mind at that precise moment would be whether to take it or report it. If you happen to be an honest person, unlike most people, you would resist the temptation and probably report it to the driver or the police. The point I am trying to make here is this. The reason why you didn't take that phone, especially if there was a possibility that you could get away with it without being noticed, would have been due to your belief on what you consider to be right or wrong. As you can see from this example, having a belief or believing in something definitely has its benefits.

One of the main benefits of beliefs in general would be in the creating of positive thinking, which really helps to bring our beliefs closer to reality.

Provides a Sense of Direction

Our belief, in general, does provide a sense of direction because it actually plays an important role in our lives today. Let's say, for instance, you believe you are a very confident person. What you will begin to notice is that you start to act confidently. For example, your body language changes, tone of voice, etc. What the majority of us fail to realize is that it's our subconscious mind that is really at work, making us act the way we act due to the belief stored in our mind. In this example you happen to have a belief that you are a confident person. What then happens is you gradually become very optimistic about who you are, in relation to your level of self-confidence. Bear in mind all this is due to the belief stored in your mind, which your subconscious picked up on.

At some stage in your life you might come across a feeling known as fear, which then gives you reasons to question your belief. This is what I call the "doubt syndrome disease". For instance, let's just say you were mistreated when you were much younger, perhaps by members of your family or a trusted friend. Furthermore, maybe someone might have said something which was very unpleasant to you, for example, "you are a loser", "you are nothing", "you are hopeless" etc. This probably made you very sad since words can have a very damaging effect on us.

Using another example, it could also be that you take pride in your physical appearance, which then makes you feel very attractive or sexy. Now, these existing beliefs that you have probably have a lot to do with why you feel so attractive in public. But imagine if someone comes along and tells you that you actually look awful. Depending on who you are, this can actually have a very bad effect on you. Most especially on your self-confidence because it would give you reason to question what you believe. During this period you are more than likely to be contaminated with the doubt syndrome disease.

A person without a strong mind, or personality, would be affected the most because it would shatter your confidence in what you believe. But if you happen to be a strong believer, with a strong personality and mind, this won't affect you as much, simply because you would see it as a challenge, trying to prove that person wrong. This is the type of attitude a strong believer would have. "An optimist sees an opportunity in every calamity, while a pessimist sees a calamity in every opportunity."

Builds Up Faith

Before we can describe faith you need to have a full understanding of what faith is. So what is faith exactly? Being brought up in a Christian family I was taught that faith is the assurance of things hoped for but yet not seen. This is my definition of faith and how I understand it, according to my beliefs. I am quite sure by now that you are beginning to see how beliefs work.

I did another survey with an entirely different type of people, whose beliefs are strictly based on what they see or have experienced in life. My goal was to find out their opinions on what they consider faith to be. According to my survey, some described faith to be a firm belief in something for which there is no evidence of its manifestation. Others, surprisingly, described it to be an act of believing in God.

But one thing I can definitely assure you of is that there are quite a lot of people in the world whose views or opinions on faith are completely different from yours or mine. This might make you wonder why. But Bertrand Russell described faith to be, "something we do not speak of when there is evidence, we do not speak of faith that two and two are four, or that the earth is round. We only speak of faith when we wish to substitute emotion for evidence."

Faith can definitely be a very challenging topic to discuss, or explain to people in general in some cases. "Faith is boundless and that which is truly holy is bound by faith" (Christopher Rowe). These are just some of the benefits of believing in something or having a belief. Thus, I am quite sure you can also see the relation between faith and beliefs.

What Really Influences Our Beliefs?

I began to find this to be a very interesting topic, especially after speaking with the majority of the people I know who belonged to a different religious faith. This happened to be not only an interesting discussion but it also proved my hypothesis at that time, because it related back to upbringing and family background.

At the age of fifteen, while I was still at secondary school, my English teacher once asked a member of the class what he would like to be at a later age in his life and why. He responded passionately by saying, "I would like to be a businessman, because my father is a businessman." This example just shows how upbringing, and family background, can really influence our beliefs.

Criticism

If you happen to be a person of purpose or just an individual who believes in something, you will definitely face critics at some stage in your life. You will also need to learn how to understand and deal with them accordingly. People criticize in general simply because they either don't understand what you believe in, or probably don't agree with it. There are quite a few factors one needs to consider, especially when trying to pinpoint the reason why critics criticize.

- People criticize out of pure jealousy/envy
- People criticize what they don't understand.

Criticizing Out of Jealousy

Most people criticize out of jealousy the majority of the time, simply because they either believe they are better than you are, or just that they deserve what you have or might have achieved. Let's take a look at an example. Let's imagine you've always dreamt of running your own business. One of the things you will come to realize is, in fact, that the people whom you thought were your true friends aren't. Also the people whom you might have thought wanted you to succeed actually don't.

These are some of the first phases you will experience. Most people tend to be jealous of successful people, just because they have achieved some of their goals, which created the success they have. You might think to yourself, but that can't be fair. You are quite right but such is life. Those who are jealous of the success of others are mainly jealous just because they can only dream of achieving the success that person might have achieved. I can guarantee you that if you are successful, or when you achieve success, you will definitely get to see this trend in some people.

This can be a painful experience in your life depending on who you are. Most of the time it starts from close friends and family, which just goes to show that no matter who you are, no matter what you might have managed to achieve, there is always a price to pay.

We also have another type of people whom I refer to as dream stealers. Their mission is to steal your dream, through discouragement, negative advice etc.

Usually people with these characteristics tend to be those who weren't as willing to take risks, weren't as determined as you were to achieve their goals. They will try to discourage you from achieving plainly out of jealousy and envy. When you look around you, try to notice the type of company most successful people keep. They usually consist of people who are also successful, simply because success breeds success. For example, when you look at celebrities today, they are known to associate with people in the same league as them; I mean fellow celebrities. You might wonder why, but it's really simple. To achieve success in life, you will also need to meet people (make contacts) and also learn from people.

If you consistently surround yourself with people who do not share the same passion or desire you have to succeed, you will only be wasting your precious time because they will slow you down through bad advice and attitude towards success. Some of the time this happens subconsciously, meaning they might not even have a clue that they are doing it. Jealousy is created through emotion, especially when it controls us. For example, "I deserve to have a car like his; if I can't have it, I see no reason why he should."

You have to be alert and aware of the company you keep in order to spot this trend in people. The greatest weapon jealous people have is discouragement, which can prevent or slow down your progression. When you first start to notice this trend, it can get a bit frustrating. The trick is to know and understand why they are doing it, and that will definitely make you feel much better. "How much better a thing it is to be envied than to be pitied" (source unknown).

I remember quite clearly when I first decided to write this book. Most of my so-called friends at that time laughed and some even tried to discourage me through negative advice. At first I was a bit upset about it, questioning myself, contemplating whether to write or not. But I soon pulled myself together as soon as I realized why they reacted the way they did. I became very determined to prove them wrong, especially through the help of using constant affirmations, such as, "I am a man of vision, I have got good ideas and I am successful." This helped to reinforce my belief, which, in return, made me a lot stronger mentally.

You might wonder how that happened. This affirmation simply changed my negative thinking into positive. For example, I developed a strong belief in myself and my capabilities up to the point whereby I found it easy to deal with my fear and any obstacles in my way.

If you happen to have a strong belief in something, for example, a goal, you must be prepared to face and deal with critics in order to get ahead. Most jealous people hate and despise anyone successful because it only reminds them that they haven't achieved the success they hope for. This makes them feel inferior and they hate it. "Wise men put their trust in ideas and not in circumstances," said Ralph Waldo Emerson.

Why People Criticize What They Don't Understand

The world is full of different types of people; some are shallow, narrow minded and ignorant. One thing I have realized is this; people with these characteristics usually become critics of some kind. They also tend to believe they have answers to everything. You will come across people like this who will challenge your beliefs because they lack understanding and are usually too proud to admit it. What they fail to realize is this; understanding is usually achieved through careful study, question asking and seeking different opinions.

A good example of this was when I first got involved in sales. My critics at that time disagreed and criticized what I did by saying all sorts of things, for example, "get a good job, this is a loser's job". They were more than likely convinced that I had lost my mind, simply because I had to work on commission, meaning that if I didn't sell, I didn't get paid. They believed working on commission just doesn't work. "One man's food is another man's poison." Always do what you think is best for you; this is my policy.

Most critics are quick to resent your ideas, beliefs or even, in some cases like mine, your chosen profession. They are quick to judge without stopping to think why you are doing what you are doing, what you are hoping to achieve from it. Some of the mistakes my critics made was not bothering to ask me any of these questions listed above. But they were quick to judge my actions just because they couldn't make any sense out of them.

Another thing you might notice is that critics, deep down in their heart, aren't really happy people. They usually moan or complain about everything instead of dealing with it, saying, for example, "I hate it when it rains. Why does it have to rain?" Most critics of success suffer from negative emotion, which then leads to negative thinking, simply because they have been unable to deal with their negative emotion.

Critics of success look for the worst things that can happen when trying to achieve success. They don't concentrate more on the good things that come with it. For instance, when I was about to start my own business, I was constantly reminded "What if it doesn't work" etc. However, some critics are good to have for our success, for example, parents and mentors. When a parent thinks a son or daughter is heading in the wrong direction the normal reaction is to question or criticize your action, until there is a justification or an understandable explanation for it. Bear in mind that their reaction is based on love, so it's really up to you to make them understand. Mentors are also very valuable simply because they possess the knowledge and experience about the field you are going into. As a result can they can lead you to the right path and show you what route not to take.

If you are constantly surrounded by negative critics it can easily put unnecessary pressure on you, to the point that you feel like giving up. During my experience with negative critics, one thing kept me going despite their opinions or views; it was one of the things my mentors taught me: "When you buy someone's opinion, be prepared to buy their lifestyle". Every single time I listened to what my critics had to say this thought always crossed my mind. Then I looked at their lifestyle – who they, are and what they stand for. This made me realize that I couldn't buy their opinion. I have always believed that I was born to be great, and great I will be, no matter how long it takes me. This was due to the fact that I have a strong belief that part of my mission in life is to contribute to the world in some way. Despite the numerous times I have been criticized, this particular belief remained unshakeable and kept me inspired, motivated and even more aggressive about hitting my goals, just to be able to look at them in the eye and confidently say, "you were wrong". This belief and my action towards hitting my goal, created an inexpressable joy and feeling in my heart, simply because I knew I was going to prove them wrong. As Abraham Lincoln said, "Most folks are as about as happy as they make up their minds to be."

Judging by my experience, I can guarantee you, when you look around you will come to realize that you are surrounded by people with great ideas that never get put into action. Because they have failed to believe in themselves, they talk less of their ideas.

And due to this, they ignore or reject potential success. The reason why most people fail to succeed is because they suffer from the disease I call the "doubt syndrome". When someone suffers from self-doubt it simply means they fail to understand that believing in one's self not only gives you the opportunity to be creative in regards to putting your ideas into practice, but it also enhances your level of determination. This, in return, will give you the unlimited will and burning desire to work towards making your dreams come true, no matter how long it takes. The will and desire you possess will see you through any negative experience you might encounter. In order to succeed in life one has to be willing to make mistakes and learn from them.

Apart from lacking self-belief, another factor that can slow you down is concentrating on too many things at the same time, or just going with the flow having no direction or goals.

As I sat there, I thought about how often we put right keys into wrong locks, and wrong keys into right locks, and right keys into locks without knowing about the slight twist to the left before the turn to the right. I was reminded of times when

I have followed the advice of an "expert" who supposedly knows the way, only to find that the directions are garbled, or that they work for the expert but not for me, and I have to find my own path through the woods.

(Eloise Ristad)

Chapter Two

Why We Believe What We Believe

When you think deeply about the reasons why we believe what we believe you only come to realize that there are quite a few factors responsible. As you read this chapter you will start to realize, and also be able to identify in your own mind, the mechanism behind what encourages us to believe what we believe. The four main factors are: upbringing; environment; peer groups and personal life experiences.

Upbringing

Between the ages of two and three a child really begins to learn from its parents, for example, learning how to talk, pronounce words, language, differentiation between the dad and mum, tone of voice, facial features etc. Also during this age period, a child really begins to develop a lot more, not only physically, but also mentally. The child also develops personality. For example, different types of mood swings when looking for but deprived of attention.

Children are known to express themselves in many ways in relation to what they want. For example, a child crying when seeking attention from parent, crying when hungry, or when deprived of something, like a toy. They sometimes make facial gestures or even in some cases act in a destructive manner just to express how they are feeling. This usually prompts the parents to action.

Children are very creative and very curious, most especially at a younger age. This is one of the reasons why parents or guardians need to keep watch on them twenty-four hours a day. As you must have heard people say, having kids and looking after them is equivalent to having a full-time job. This statement is actually true, ask any parent.

As a child gets older, the child also gets wiser. They continually learn adaptable characteristics from the parents by observing their personalities or habits. For instance, when a child watches, he/she observes the activities of their surroundings. For example, a child learns to wash his/her hands before sitting to eat at the dining table simply because the action was carried out by the parent/guardian.

Why? During this period in a child's life, he or she happens to be at a stage of learning, which most people refer to as the learning process. During this period the parent is subconsciously seen as a role model, a teacher to learn from. This then creates in the child a strong eagerness and willingness to learn. Children, in particular, find everything around them amusing and interesting. This then triggers that part of the brain which is responsible for stimulating or arousing curiosity. Children, as you know already, are naturally adventurous. But the only thing stopping them from being too adventurous at that age is something called a parent or guardian, which is a good thing. You are probably wondering why am saying this.

Let's look at this in the right perspective. When a child becomes too adventurous at an early age the possibility of the child leading him/herself into harm's way is very high. Bear in mind that a child at that age doesn't understand why there should be a limit to what he/she can or should do. For example, let's imagine a child makes an attempt to run after and chase pigeons just to have fun. But at the same time, the street happens to be very busy and full of motorists passing by continually. Due to this, the child gets held back by the parent/guardian.

The natural reaction of the child is to either cry, or to behave unpleasantly to show the parent how displeased or unhappy he/she is. This reaction usually consists of body language. Due to this, the common reaction of the parent/guardian would be to offer an explanation to the child, to help him/her understand the reason for their action. This brings us to the "why factor".

As you must have gathered so far, the why factor in this scenario was to protect the child from any form of danger, such as getting hit by a moving vehicle etc. At this point the child would have learnt an important lesson about safety and precaution. Subconsciously, this information would be stored in the subconscious mind of the child bearing in mind that the child sees the parent as a role model, someone to look up to and learn from.

When the child eventually gets to a much older age, for example primary school stage, one thing is certain: he/she would still remember the important lesson on safety and precaution, taught by the parent or guardian. The lesson would always be in the memory of the child, and it can be triggered when facing the same situation. For example, if a child as been brought up to look left and right before crossing the road, he/she would always remember this piece of information whenever attempting to cross the road in the future, simply because the child by now believes it's the right thing to do.

This is just some of the important information the child has learnt from the parent/guardian at an early age, due to the fact that, as humans, we have a complex brain, which stores valid information into our subconscious minds that can be retrieved whenever needed. This process is best described as the input and output of data. You might wonder why we don't usually store less important information. This is simply because we usually only retain information that is, or could be, of great benefit to us. For example our religious beliefs, our right from wrong, our birthdays. This has a lot to do with our upbringing, because we tend to believe what we are taught as a kid.

These are just some of the other examples with regards to why we believe what we believe, and how reactive we can be towards them. "Teach a child how to grow, and when he grows older he would not depart from it."

Environment

One of the other important factors that you will realize, as you study more about the reason why we believe what we believe, is that of our environment, most especially our social surroundings, which has a lot of impact on us as we develop into adults. For instance, if a child grows up in a hostile environment, where he/she constantly witnesses men maltreating women, kids taking drugs, or indulging in theft, he/she would have a higher probability rate of being influenced by the environment and possibly accepting and believing it to be the norm.

I once read about some of the major reasons why children get bullied at school. To my surprise some of the main reasons that were highlighted were due to:

- Race/nationality
- Accent/pronunciation
- Family background.

Kids usually get bullied at school by naïve children for various reasons, for example, lack of good upbringing. Usually kids who bully others not only reflect images of themselves but also of their childhood experiences, which mainly have a lot to do with their parents and environment.

Accent

Many kids also get bullied for having a different type of accent, just because other kids find it unacceptable for pronunciation to sound different. Bullies are just products of their environment, which consist of their homes, friends, neighbourhood etc. All these factors have a major effect on them.

According to statistics, the main areas or neighbourhoods with a high or an increasing crime rate are usually areas with a high percentage of poverty. This basically indicates and explains why most of these children do not have a good educational background or upbringing. Most kids lack manners because they weren't brought up in a way that would enable them to become productive adults in the future. Some kids even bully others out of jealousy because they feel, if I can't have what he/she has, or if I can't speak like he/she does then no one will or should.

You might wonder why this is so. One thing you have to remember is that they believe it's the right thing to do or the right way to behave. I am sure you can now see, in more detail, how important our beliefs are, and most especially why we believe what we believe. Now, let's just imagine for a second why children or bullies act this way. Thinking about this deeply, you will realize that something's responsible; there isn't any smoke without fire, as you must have guessed.

Relating this to the environment, it may be that the kid saw his or her friend bully others, or perhaps he or she saw their father or mother trying to dominate or control the other, and accepted this as the norm. I grew up in a school environment where this was a way of life to the students. The school I attended is based in the south of London, near Kennington. I witnessed a lot of bullying, most especially by my fellow students, who only did it to fit in, not because they particularly enjoyed it. The motto was basically bully or get bullied. Anyone who basically didn't want to be bullied had to become one if they wanted to avoid trouble. This almost became like a culture, "If you can't beat them, join them". This happened to be a problem for me, because I had a different upbringing and opposed their beliefs and actions. Being brought up in a nice family, I was taught that bullying was wrong. And due to my non-negotiable attitude in relation to what they wanted me to do, and expected me to do, I usually found myself in tight situations, just because I believed it was wrong and was bold enough to express it.

While I was at secondary school, bullying was seen in the eyes of others to be a cool thing to do, especially if you wanted to fit in or become well known or popular. One question that might be going through your mind could be: "But some kids who come from good families bully people as well, especially from the environment just described." This is quite true and I am not in any way trying to overrule this point. The point I am trying to make here is really simple. The environment a person surrounds themselves in tends to have a major impact on their daily lives, most especially on their behaviour pattern, how they think, react, or do things in general. This is simply based on their beliefs, which, in this case, happens to be due to their environment.

I have actually come across kids who come from a poor family background but yet were still well mannered at school, in regards to behaving appropriately. I have also come across children from a wealthy family background whose behaviour happens to be very poor. This only proves that the environment we surround ourselves by influences us for better or for worse, one way or another.

Judging from my observation on why we believe what we believe, in relation to our environment, I can confidently say that if a person surrounds him/herself in a more positive environment the chances of that person growing up to be a productive adult in the future are great. Using this same scenario in the opposite direction, I would say if a person surrounds him/herself in a more negative environment then the chances of becoming a productive adult in the future are very slim.

Family Background

This is a major factor that keeps recurring when trying to find out why we believe what we believe, and the factors responsible. You might be wondering why. This is really simple. Let's say, for instance, a child grows up watching his/her parents arguing all the time or fighting constantly. Judging by this, the child would definitely have some difficulty while growing up into an adult because he or she would find it strange not to behave in a similar pattern, especially when he or she comes across people who do not behave in the same way.

Another example is a child who grows up witnessing their parents being physically aggressive to one another during or after a heated discussion. One thing that can be almost certain is the fact that the child would grow up believing that's the right way to act or behave in a situation where both parties happen to be upset. All this comes back to the fact that the child sees both parents as a role model, someone to learn from and to look up to.

Let's look back a bit into the history of psychopaths. One thing you need to understand when considering this is that they did what they did because they have somehow made themselves believe it's the right thing to do. We can see clearly from their actions that they are not in control of their minds any longer because they simply can't differentiate right from wrong. One thing is definitely for sure, something must have pushed them to the limit, such as depression, being treated unfairly, mental or physical abuse etc.

In most cases, when looking at what made such people the way they are, the answer lies in their history, their family background or upbringing.

Peer Groups

While we are still developing, we tend to pick up good and bad habits, most especially bad habits. Some of the reason why we actually do this, even though we might not realize it at the moment it occurs, is simply because we have been influenced or are being influenced by peer groups, such as friends etc. This usually clouds our judgment, preventing us from thinking clearly about our actions.

We usually spend most of our free time mainly with our peer groups at a younger age. We are very quick to copy one another. A good example would be to imagine yourself back at primary school. Imagine your friend's father just bought him a new pair of shoes. What you will begin to realize is that you want the same, if not better. This becomes very important to you to the point whereby you won't feel happy or content until you get it.

Another good example would be kids who hang around with other kids who smoke. What usually happens is that because his/her friend smokes, there is a probability, perhaps quite high, that the other kid would want to try it out of curiosity, simply because his/her friend has.

These are some examples of how we are influenced by our peer groups, especially at a younger age. Another example is ecstasy. Most people take it regularly and are fine, even though they know is bad for them. The real danger usually falls upon the other friend who takes the drug out of curiosity, wanting to fit in. This starts from the motivation given by the ringleader. "Come on, you can do it, there is nothing to it." This friend might happen to take the drug for the first time and drop dead as a result. This just goes to show the type of influence peer groups have on us when dealing with our beliefs, especially why we believe what we believe.

Personal Life Experiences

This is another important factor that one needs to look at when trying to evaluate the reason why we tend to believe what we believe. For example, a person can grow up hating being around lots of people due to past life experiences. This clearly shows that the abuse experienced has left a mental scar which troubles the mind of the individual, making the person feel uncomfortable around a lot of people, or people in general. This usually happens once the person has convinced him/herself that it is wrong to be among people.

Our personal experiences in life have a great deal of psychological effect on us, most especially while we are still at a younger age. Most people spend their lives not ever figuring out how personal life experiences can contribute to our mental beliefs, which we usually refuse to question, but accept.

Another example is, let's say, for instance, everyone you've loved and trusted had, at some time, proved that they can't be trusted, or weren't who they made you think they were. In a situation like this, especially if it has occurred several times, it's really easy to develop a belief that people can't be trusted even though we know everyone is different. Most people, when faced with some disappointment at some stage in their life, for example a failed business, failed marriages etc., usually tend to give up because it is the easier thing to do as we all know, and also because they create and develop a personal belief based on their situation which then keeps or prevents them from being optimistic or being able to figure out what the problem was, or where it went wrong or started from. Relating this to a failed marriage, one example would be, "My marriage failed because marriage is not for me. It just doesn't work". Another example would be, "My business failed because I am not a good entrepreneur."

These are some of the negative attitudes and beliefs that most people develop and nurture which prevent them from succeeding. We need to take control of our negative emotions in order to solve our problems and achieve what we want. In most cases people get stuck in the same situation over and over again, failing to realize or determine the main cause of the problem. And as a result, they eventually lose focus or the inner drive, which encourages us to keep going. Instead they keep on blaming themselves, their situation and others.

This process usually continues until it becomes a concrete part of their belief. For example, they continue to say to themselves, "I can't do this, I can only be successful if am lucky." One thing most of us still don't realize is that our problems get worse from the point we stop believing in ourselves. We are our number one enemy, when we fail to belief in ourselves first, before trying to solve a problem or achieve anything.

This is one of the reasons why I believe strongly that our life experiences do play a major part in, and in most cases have an effect on, what we choose to not to believe or believe.

Chapter Three

What Self-belief Really is and How it Works

Self-belief is having total confidence in one's self, and the ability to do anything realistic once you are determined and focused. Self-belief can also be described as an ego-booster that encourages us to trust ourselves more, which then provides us with the motivational drive that we need to achieve our personal goal.

How it Works

Self-belief really works in various ways or forms, for example, in our behaviour. People act in a certain way in public when meeting new people. It might have crossed your mind to question why that is. This is simply because we tend to believe that it is the right thing to do. Let's use a little bit of imagination to make this example a lot clearer. Now, imagine yourself meeting someone for the first time. Subconsciously, your behaviour, pattern changes. Why? This is mainly because you are trying to create an image or an impression about you towards the other person. Thinking about this, what we are really doing is we are becoming an actor; trying to be who we are not. For example, the majority of people only get involved in a task that they believe they posses a high efficacy in. And also they usually avoid those tasks in which they posses a low efficacy. This also might make you wonder why people act that way.

First this happens simply because they fail to believe in themselves. They create a belief that they can't be good at such tasks, just because they happen to have low efficacy. Second, people with such an attitude fail to understand what I call the "law of perfection", which states that practice makes perfect. By simply either acquiring some or more knowledge about those tasks in which your efficacy is low, you will automatically see that you get better and better, even if the improvement is gradual.

Benefits of self-belief include:

- It creates perceived self-efficacy
- It creates a persistent spirit/attitude

Creating Perceived Efficacy

This actually works like magic. It helps in shaping casual things, for example if you happen to have failed at something you wanted to get right. It helps you not to focus too much on the negative side, but more on the positive side of things, which in return gives you hope and the willingness to try again and get it right. You could say, "If I had put in more effort I would have done much better."

Creating a Persistent Spirit/Attitude

Creating a persistent spirit and attitude helps a lot, most especially when we are trying to achieve something. A typical example to use would be boxing. You must have seen various situations whereby the two boxers are fighting for a championship title. Both are really tired but still they keep on fighting to the end because what they are looking to achieve is to win the fight, which is what keeps them going even though they might be badly injured. The fear of losing to them is just too great to comprehend.

At the end of the fight, it's either a draw or one boxer has to win, either by points or whosoever caused the most damage. When the winner is eventually declared, the other boxer at this point obviously realizes that he/she has lost. It is at this point when attitude really kicks in. Despite the fight they usually hug and make up, which shows a good sportsmanship spirit. This is just an example I am using to demonstrate the persistent spirit, that is, fighting to the end, not ever giving up. This also demonstrates a good attitude, losing the fight but still being optimistic and looking forward to the next challenge. "You can lose a battle but still win a war" (source unknown).

There is actually nothing wrong in setting a goal and not achieving it because you will at least get close to it. But there is something wrong with a person who doesn't have a goal to achieve in the first place. You might disagree with me but that's my own opinion. One thing I have come to realize in life, based on my own personal experiences and others', is that the only thing that keeps us sane in this insane world is the ability to believe in something, or having a goal to achieve.

Chapter Four

Being Open-Minded to Our Beliefs

Day in, day out, we all come across people who aren't open-minded about their beliefs. If you wonder why, then you really need to study this chapter carefully. Most people suffer from what I call the "fixed belief syndrome". This has a lot to do with the mindset of individuals, for example, at some stage in your life, you might have come across an individual who happened to have a fantastic idea but was too scared to bring it into reality by doing something about it. It usually becomes that person's belief that "it wouldn't work", before he had even tried. The person had negative "self-talk", such as "No one will take me seriously", "Due to competition it would not work", "People will laugh at me", "I am not good enough".

Some might even have an idea that can make him/her financially independent. But usually they will laugh off the idea or just ignore it and let it pass by, simply because they do not believe in themselves first and foremost, let alone the idea. All of these are typical examples of fixed beliefs. It is exactly this type of belief that keeps us from achieving or discovering our full potential.

Another reason has to do with change. Most of us are constantly scared of change because we tend to believe it is a bad thing. We don't usually see it as turning out to be good, simply because of our comfort zone. People are constantly scared of change for these reasons and most adapt an attitude of "I would rather stick to what I know". It is this type of belief, which we create, that is one of the reasons people miss out on good opportunities. "People miss out on a good opportunity because it's dressed in an overall and looks like work" (source unknown).

The majority of us are scared to come out of our comfort zone and as a result we use it as an excuse for getting complacent. What most of us fail to realize is that change is inevitable, simply because with change new experiences are born, new achievement, wealth, happiness etc. For example, if mankind never changed, we would still be living in caves like animals. And we would never have found civilization.

We all know that, as humans, we have a complex brain, which can serve us in a positive way or in a negative way, depending on how we use it. When we become open-minded to our beliefs, we send signals to the brain, which then creates more room to learn or absorb, and analyze new information, for example, new ideas, different ways of viewing things in general etc.

Chapter Five

How to be Open-Minded in Our Beliefs

Creating an Open Mind

To create an open mind, one needs to learn and adapt a habit of questioning things. Why is this? How did this happen? Where did this come from? And so on.

Observation

In order to enhance your level of open-mindedness towards your belief, you need to observe and really study your belief, or what you believe in. The next step would be to do a comparison with other beliefs, while using all five senses to note any deviation. The best way to do this is by comparing logically and accurately.

By doing so, you will start to see the benefits. For example, you will develop more awareness towards other beliefs. You will also be able to notice similarities, if there are any. Being open-minded in our beliefs has a lot of benefits and few disadvantages. For example, if you are not open-minded, but remain ignorant, you might never know what you could learn.

Being an Independent Thinker

This happens to have many definitions. Some describe it to be the ability to rely just on one's own thinking, without depending on others. An independent thinker can also be described as a person who makes sense of the world around him/her, simply based on self-observation or personal encounters and life experiences. Let's now relate this to being open-minded in our beliefs.

To become an independent thinker, you need to have some of the following characteristics:

- Ability to question things
- Being pro-active
- Critical thinking
- Creative explanations.

Ability to Question Things

When we question things, we are, in a way, being open-minded because we are not taking whatever we have been told or taught as valid fact.

For example, your class teacher tells you the earth is round; you respond by asking a question. How do you know it is round, not flat? Let's imagine the lecturer now goes on to explain why and provides proof to back up his/her statement.

Bearing in mind that you responded that way due to the uncertainty that you had, this then made you very curious and unconvinced, to the point where you had to have more information to convince you that the earth is round not flat. In this case that's what the lecturer had to do, in order to convince you or make you believe.

Being open-minded is not a bad thing but a good thing because it makes you aware of the unknown whereby you then gain more knowledge in general. When we believe in something, it is more like a process of conditioning our subconscious mind into accepting a particular or certain type of information. Our mind then stores it as valid information, which is more like a programming process.

The mind is the most powerful tool we have as human beings. It's what makes us who we are, our personalities, how we portray ourselves, think, or do things. To be open-minded in our beliefs, what we need to do is to feed our subconscious mind with information that will challenge what we believe. The best way to do this is to use a lot of affirmation.

Affirmation is basically a process of programming the subconscious mind with information that will challenge it. Once a question mark is raised about our beliefs in our minds, we start to question them. When this happens, what we are really doing, indirectly, is being open-minded to our beliefs.

Being Pro-active

As an independent thinker who is open-minded or wants to be open-minded to his/her beliefs, pro-activeness is essential. You might wonder why, or probably wonder what I mean by this. Being pro-active is an ability to take action towards achieving a specific goal or target strictly based on independent thinking. For example, a man wants to know or find out whether what he's been brought up to believe, is actually the truth or not. What he then decides to do is to carry out research, and to study all that he needs to know about his belief.

He then also has to relate it to his own personal life experiences and others as well. In this example, what the man is doing here is being pro-active. He didn't wait around for anyone to tell him what to do next, or how to go about it. He simply just used his own initiative and off he went. This clearly shows his pro-activeness.

How to be Pro-active in Our Beliefs

When you think deeply about being pro-active in your beliefs you will realize that it's a simple process once mastered. This process can be carried out not only by being open-minded in what we believe but also by taking the necessary action towards finding out the information needed. This is what I refer to as the first stage.

Second Stage

At the point when all the information required has been gathered, that's when you arrive at the second stage. The next thing to do is to carry out a thorough study of the information you have been able to gather together before beginning your quest. When this is done, what you will start to discover is how much you never knew about that particular belief that you had. For example, if you once believed that there wasn't a supreme being (God) and, as a result, decided to satisfy your curious mind by doing a survey, research, or perhaps a careful study about the history and origin of the universe, one of the first things you will realize, is that you didn't know as much as you thought you did. This would then make you more curious about finding out more, until you get your answers eventually.

Benefits

When we develop an act of being pro-active to our beliefs, we gain some benefits. It helps the curious mind to search for what we might have presumed to be the truth, right or wrong, for example, if you had believed all your life that you were born to be great, due to the fact that your parents told you so as a kid.

What usually happens depending on how strong your beliefs are, is that you will start to search for greatness in many ways, simply because you have developed that belief that it's your birthright. The important thing I want you to look at here is this. At this point you are quite aware that if you are to find greatness, it won't just come to you – you have to achieve it. A good example would be a person who continually moans and complains that he/she is broke and has no money, when all he/she has to do is go in search for money by working etc.

When you go in search of something you believe you truly deserve wholeheartedly, especially when you've developed a strong belief that you truly deserve it, you will definitely get it, as long as you also work towards it even though it might take time. But why? Determination and self-belief definitely.

The reason why I am saying this is because I have seen it work for many people, including myself. When we become pro-active, it gets us into action. When we are in motion, the only thing that keeps us going, despite any obstacles we might face, is nothing other than our determination to get or achieve what we believe is rightfully ours.

Relating this back to the example of you believing you were born to be great, the only thing that got you to take action to search for that greatness was your pro-activeness. You didn't wait to be told what to do, or how to go about it, the decision was strictly made by you, because you became or are an independent thinker.

Most people you are likely to come across are not pro-active but reactive. The reason why I am saying this is because I have met a lot of people, as you probably have, who turn out to be reactive.

Reactive People

This type of people wait until they are told what to do before they act. They also fit into the category of people who wait until their situation changes, when they know it is going to change anyway, before they even make an effort. For example, most people complain that they hate their job, but never take the necessary action needed to make their job more enjoyable or to find another until they are finally dismissed.

Another example would be a company director addressing the company staff about a need to lay off a good few people unless they are willing to get a payout or develop new skills. What is clear is that eventually most of these people still get laid off or made redundant just because they have failed to change, for example, by developing that new skill needed or finding another well-paid job before the crunch time arrives for people to get laid off.

That's why I call them reactive, they wait to be pushed before moving. The majority of people are reactive due to laziness, low self-esteem, lack of self-belief, depression and anxiety. In a way these are significant problems to have but, despite this, they can be solved if only the person could take the first step of believing. This is what I refer to as the thin line between being pro-active and reactive.

Pro-active people are usually leaders, ambitious people and goal setters. Reactive people are usually lazy, followers, people who act on impulse. One other benefit in relation to being pro-active our beliefs, is that it helps us in achieving things we have dreamt, desired or believe we will achieve. For example, let's imagine you are an athlete in a 200-metre race. Also you strongly believe that you are the best person and deserve to win. What you would do prior to the race is prepare vigorously by practising physically and mentally to win. When the day then finally arrives, if you don't win, you will have at least tried your best and come close.

This is just a theoretical explanation of the power of self-belief, when it comes to achieving goals. But if you win, your "ego" would only grow bigger and stronger because you've just proved what you believed would happen by winning the race, which then brings your belief to reality.

Question: what do you think helped you in the race? It's definitely self-belief, pro-activeness, determination and talent.

Below are some important questions that might cross your mind:

1 Do people with high self-esteem always value themselves? Yes, but they sometimes face situations that can create doubt in their mind.

2 Do secure people ever feel insecure? Yes, because everyone is insecure about something, deep down.

3 Does having self-confidence mean you are full of yourself? Not exactly, it simply shows that you believe in yourself and are aware of your capabilities or full potential.

4 Is it possible to doubt one's belief? Of course, circumstances can play a major role.

5 Is it a good or bad thing to be over-confident? It's bad for us to be over-confident, because we can slowly become ignorant and arrogant, thinking we know it all.

Chapter Six

The Role Self-belief Plays in our Lives

Self-belief plays an important role in our lives, especially in today's world. We've got countries going to war, simply because their leaders or their government believe strongly that's the only way to get rid of any threat. One thing I want you to bear in mind is this: the leaders or the government wouldn't have authorized the decision to launch an attack on a rival country if they didn't believe in themselves first that they would win, whether it is the right thing, or lawful thing to do, or perhaps is the only way to protect their country from a possible future attack. You might find this rather confusing, but as you read you will begin to understand the point I am driving at.

Let's look at the situation between Afghanistan and America. The man known as Osama Bin Laden, who happens to be a leader of the notorious terrorist group, believed he was doing the right thing by attacking America due to his religious beliefs.

When you think about it, he must have believed in himself first to be able to lead his followers and encourage them to carry out the disastrous acts which took place on 11 September 2001. Using this example, I am sure you can now begin to see some of the role self-belief plays, or can play, in our lives.

Self-belief plays a very significant role in our lives because it can lead us to many destinations, whether it be a positive or a negative destination. It all depends on the individual. I have seen and heard of so many cases where self-belief has led many to a bad or good destination. For example, Sir Richard Branson; he is one of the most successful people that deserve applause. He started from nothing to become a multimillionaire, owning over two hundred companies. One thing is certain: he wouldn't have achieved any of this if he didn't believe, first of all, in the number one thing, which is himself. Once again, you can now see the role self-belief played in his life. Most of the time, people who believe in themselves end up becoming productive adults in the future.

I am quite sure you must have either read or come across a few successful people. One thing they all have in common is self-belief, as you might have already read in the second chapter of this book, where I talked about the benefits of self-belief, including the fact that it creates high self-efficacy etc.

When you look around or speak to successful people, especially those who started from nothing, one thing you will realize is that one of the fundamental key factors to their success lies in self belief being the most important factor, and also the ability to have a persistent spirit and a good attitude.

When you are persistent, you keep going even in the toughest of situations, whereas most other people would have given up. Having a good attitude, as we know, helps to keep the fire, the desire inside of you, burning, simply because you will remain an optimistic person even a in bad situation. This is what I refer to as using the right "success psychology"; by using this method you will gradually start to develop a winner's characteristics. What do winners do best? Win. "Quitters never win, and winners never quit" (source unknown).

Despite this example and quotation, the fact remains that in order to succeed in whatever you are doing, you really ought to believe in yourself first. Another role self-belief plays in our lives is in the giving of hope, determination, personal encouragement, for example, "I am good at this", "I can achieve this", "I will succeed no matter what" etc.

When you continually focus and use all these affirmations you will gradually become stronger inside, and also end up achieving your goal, no matter how long it takes. "When the going gets tough, the tough get going."

Nelson Mandela was arrested and jailed for a long time simply due to his beliefs. You might wonder what kept him sane all those years. It is really simple. He had a vision, a goal, which, even though it took him a long time, he accomplished. That's one of the characteristics of a great person. Nelson Mandela's goal was to dismantle discrimination between races in South Africa, so that there wouldn't be segregation between races any more. He had this vision, and he strongly believed in himself that he would and could achieve it, no matter how long it took him. Due to his belief he got into a lot of trouble with the government of his country at that time. He was finally arrested and jailed for twenty-seven years because he opposed the government behind segregation, due to his strong belief which was against it. He was eventually released, with his goal already achieved through the help of his followers and supporters. He also became South Africa's president for a while, before he decided to step down. This is also another example which shows you the important role self-belief plays in our lives. "The greatest glory in living is not in never falling, but rising every time you fall" (Nelson Mandela).

We all have desires, goals, dreams that we would love to have come to pass. But we remain in a dream world instead of living our dream. This happens, not because we lack talent, ability, or knowledge, we simply fail to believe in ourselves which is what would give us the confidence and strength to make our dreams come true.

When you look at footballers, athletes, boxers, they all prepare themselves to win before winning. They prepare themselves mentally as well as physically before playing that match, or before fighting that opponent etc. Our mindset has a lot of effect when it comes to the results we achieve in life, whether it is in our professional life or personal life. When we create a strong belief that we can do or achieve something, we usually do. When we believe we can't do something, or that we are not good enough or can't afford something etc, we usually can't or won't. This might puzzle your mind.

Believing strongly that you can actually achieve or do something automatically sends signals to your brain, which then supplies your mind with answers, or different ideas on how to make or bring that belief to reality. For example, you see a nice car that you would love to have, and you believe strongly that you can have it. What then happens is almost magical. Your mind starts working out a route; you can take to make those dreams come true, regardless of your current situation. A good example, you start to develop ideas on how you can raise the money to purchase the car, if you need a better or well-paid job that will enable you to afford it. Maybe you need a loan etc. When you look around you, you can see clearly different types of vehicles, clothing design, products etc. All this started from a thought in someone's mind, but only materialized because the person who thought of the idea in the first place believed in him/herself, and the idea, and also was confident enough to bring it to reality.

This is yet another example of the role self-belief plays in our lives. Most people you come across probably don't think in this way and that is why they achieve less, simply because they tend to be critical thinkers they criticize their own ideas before ever thinking or asking themselves whether it is feasible or not.

The main reason behind this is simply because they lack one of the most important ingredients, which is self-belief. Most people are quick to say, "It just isn't something I can do", "It just wouldn't work" etc. When you say these things to yourself continually, it then becomes your reality because you believe it. Instead of thinking this way, you need to adapt a habit of reciting positive thoughts to your- self all the time, every day. When you think of an idea, take time to view it and give it a try before ignoring it. Learn to block out negative thoughts or emotions by simply replacing them with positive ones. For example, you can think of your dream house, where you want to be in the next five years, your dream car, desired lifestyle. Imagine yourself doing these things, enjoying the joy it brings to the fullest. This, I can guarantee you, will get rid of that negative energy at that moment. As you become good at this, you will feel more confident about yourself and what you are looking to achieve. You will begin to trust your intuition a lot more than before. You will also, more importantly, begin to see results.

We all have a unique quality, idea etc. in us but the only way we can really discover it is by tapping into the source (imagination). Imagination is a very powerful thing because it expands our thinking, gives us clues, and can lead us to solutions. For example, if you imagine what you wouldn't want your life to be like, that means you should know what you would like it to be like.

Many people study for years at a profession they believed would provide them with the security they need in life. But despite this they still remain unhappy and feel miserable and unsatisfied. But imagine doing something you love doing, making a living out of it. How good do you think you will feel? Great. "Imagination is more important than knowledge," Albert Einstein said.

Most people spend their whole life doing something they hate doing, just to make a living or get by. They do this based on their belief of self-limitation, and some others believe that this is due to their circumstances or past experience in life, or even lack of knowledge in a specific area of interest. They tend to believe they can't do something based on these facts.

We have the most important and powerful tool, which is the human mind. All we need to do is learn how to use it wisely to our own advantage and simply have faith or trust in it. There is nothing realistic in this world that we as humans want but can't achieve. If we really have the desire, will, determination and self-belief we can and eventually will get it. "Life is like a ten-speed bicycle, most of us have gears we never use"(Charles M. Schulz).

I remember quite clearly when I decided to write this book. Most of the people I know laughed and some even believed I should just stick to what I know. There was one particular thing they failed to realize, which was the key to success. I knew from an early age, through my mentors and personal experiences, that the key to success is based mainly on knowledge and attitude. For example, let's just imagine your idea of success is to become a great salesman in the future. This then means you would have to acquire some general and relevant knowledge about sales, and what it will take to be that great salesman you've always wanted to be. Using this example, one of the things I want you to realize is that knowledge is the key. If you want to become that great salesman, you must be prepared to learn the following:

1 Patience
2 To take constructive criticism
3 To deal with rejection and not take it personally
4 To sell your personality
5 To relate to people, especially customers
6 To believe in yourself, to build confidence
7 Firm belief in the product/services being sold.

By learning all of this, you will eventually become what you've learnt because you will practise it and, as we all know, practice makes perfect.

Attitude is another important factor, which helps us to succeed in life. With the right attitude a person can go far. Having a great attitude, especially a very positive one, is like having the petrol tank of a car filled up. This would obviously make the car run more smoothly and effectively.

So What Exactly is Attitude?

Most people when asked would tell you that it's got a lot to do with your personality, how you think, or react to things or situations. My career background is in sales, whereby I sold products and services on behalf of blue chip clients such as, Virgin Energy, National Power gas/electricity, private medical insurance (through Universal Provident), Telco Global Communications etc. I had to go through a lot of training when I first got started in sales, because it was completely new to me. I previously worked for McDonald's and slowly worked my way up into a management position; then I left, about three years later, and got involved in sales.

When I first started sales, I found it very odd, simply because it was a new field to me. We usually had training every day on how to sell to customers, while at the same time relating to them. The hardest part for me then was dealing with rejection. I learnt to deal with it quickly enough once I realized that if I didn't I would only be hurting my own pocket.

I learnt a lot about attitude, something I would never have stopped to think about in the past. After being in sales for a year, I was able to come up with my own definition of what I understand attitude to be, mainly based on my sales experience. Attitude, in my opinion, is the ability to deal with frustration or rejection. This definition came about when I was working door to door, pitching to people randomly on the street.

I had to go through a lot of negatives before eventually coming across the positive customers, who seemed to be interested in what I was selling. I usually would have to speak to a minimum of three hundred people a day, just to be able to sell to four. This usually made me a £140 a day, based on the fact that I worked on 100% commission only.

Positive Customers

These are people who would listen to what you have to say about the product or service you are trying to sell. And the majority of the time, if it sounds good and they are convinced, they would buy.

Negative Customers

Those I refer to as negative customers come under the categories of people who tend to be rude or impolite towards me, even though they know I am only trying to present them with products/services they might benefit from. "The only good is knowledge, and the only evil is ignorance" (Socrates).

Looking at this from your point of view, you are probably wondering why I didn't give up. That's the power of self-belief. I have always had a dream, which is to one day run my own profit and loss company. I saw sales as an opportunity to do this. Once in a while, being only human with feelings, I do feel like giving up, but only one thing kept me going – none other than my creator God, and my burning desire to succeed.

Sales, in general, has taught me a lot about the relationship between setting a goal and hitting it. This simply required a strong belief in one's self and a great deal of patience. There is one theory that I learnt in sales, which I still use today and value very much when it comes to tackling any problem or dealing with any obstacles

Law Of Averages

This basically states that the more negativity you come across, the closer you will get to your positive. This can also be explained by saying that for every bad situation you face, maybe in your relationships, business etc., there will always be a better day so long as you stay hopeful. Every single time I feel like my patience is running out, I simply think about my goals, and I recite the law of averages theory time and time again, until I start to feel reassured.

Once again this example just goes to show the power of belief and the magnificent role it plays in our lives. Also, another good thing about the role self-belief plays in our lives is that once you achieve whatever you've been working towards you will feel so good inside and as a result this will increase your motivation towards your next project or goal.

This can also make you feel like a hero, unstoppable, especially when you meet new people or speak to new people. They will be able to sense if you believe in yourself or not, through subliminal messages. People sense this through your confidence, behaviour, the way you speak and what you say. When you go for an interview, the interviewer can tell if the interviewee is confident through tone of voice, body language, and how he/she responds to the question being asked. For example, the interviewer might ask, "Why should

I give you the job?" If you were to respond by saying, "Because I think I would be good at it," this automatically shows lack of confidence and self-belief.

These little things count because they reflect little things about us, such as personality etc. I went to a business network seminar once. The guest speaker happened to be a very successful businessman, whose topic that day was about how to create the right impression. He started off by saying, in order to create the right impression, that you need, first of all, to believe in yourself and what you are trying to do. He then went further, saying that people judge each other within the first thirty seconds of meeting. Image, which is mainly how you look etc., is important. He went on further to explain this point more precisely by saying, "If it looks like a duck, quacks like a duck, what must it be? A duck."

Chapter Seven

How the Power of Self-belief Can Lead to Success

Before you can understand how the power of self-belief can lead to success, you first of all need to understand what success really is or means to you. Everyone has a different understanding and definition of what they perceive success to be. This really comes down to the individual aspiring for success. For example, success to some people is having good health, having a well-paid job, having a big house or a very expensive car. This is just an example of how people view success and how their opinions vary from one another. I was once told by one of my mentors that to set a goal and achieve it you have to know what the goal is and understand how you are going to achieve it. In other words, I was being told to identify what I want and how I am going to get it before I set out to get what I want. This is a very true statement. If you don't know what you want and how you are going to go about getting it before setting out to get it you just going to keep going around in circles and this will usually take double the time, if not triple. "For a man who has lost is way, every way is a way" (source unknown).

When you listen to, read or study successful people you will come to realize that they believe in themselves. Believing in one's self creates inner strength, inner power. With strength you can endure pain, obstacles, problems etc. One needs a tremendous amount of strength to succeed. This type of strength usually consists of mental strength, emotional strength and spiritual strength.

Mental Strength

This is a process of mind developing. To create mental toughness, you need to believe in yourself, always staying positive; view problems as challenges; have the burning desire to succeed. Mental strength has a lot to do with our imagination. The stronger our imagination is, the quicker our minds develop and adapt. Mental strength is a skill that should be learnt in order to succeed. Some examples are the use of constant:

1 Visualization
2 Affirmation
3 Education
4 Association
5 Action.

Visualization

This is an important skill, and can be difficult to learn at an early stage. Some people think or imagine in pictures while other people think in words or shapes.

When you imagine or think in pictures you are said to have a photographic brain.

Visualization is a process of forming and painting pictures in one's mind. For example, let's just imagine your goal is to buy a house. If you then imagine yourself buying that house, living in it, enjoying the feeling of being the owner etc., you are said to be visualizing. One of my mentors used to say to me, "If you can see it, you can have it, if you can feel it, you can definitely touch it." This might sound strange to you, but I can assure you it's true.

We all desire something or someone. Before we get what we want, the idea of having what we want first crosses our mind. This is the first step. By visualizing we paint a picture of the idea, imagining it coming to pass. This usually creates a strange but nice feeling inside; I am sure you are beginning to get the picture by now.

Affirmation

This is more like a method of training the mind, or programming the mind, to respond to certain things. It is more to do with our subconscious mind. For example, you might be taking an exam, which you failed previously and have been told you will have to retake. If you say "I am never going to pass the exam", what you are really doing basically, is criticizing yourself through negative self-talk and, as a result, your subconscious picks up on it. This might also seem strange to you, but it is actually true. Using this scenario, if you re-take the exam the probability of you failing the exam will be even greater, simply because you have managed to convince yourself, through negative self-criticism, that you won't pass. And as a result you won't be keen on studying to pass anyway.

When we constantly criticize ourselves every time we make mistakes we are basically harming ourselves mentally because our subconscious minds picks up on it as a command and will, as a result, do whatever it takes to bring it as close to reality as possible. A good example would be if you believe you are a shy person, and you constantly say that to yourself. What will then happen is this. You will begin to act as if you are shy, through your behaviour pattern. Slowly your self-esteem deteriorates. That's the power of affirmation.

The reverse is what successful people do. They say positive things like "I am good at this", "All I need to do is study more, work harder", "I am a winner". Successful people use the skill of affirmation in a positive manner to their advantage and that's why they achieve good results.

Like the Bible says, you reap what you sow. So if you always use negative affirmation, you will get negative results. But when you use positive affirmation instead, you will receive positive results. You can't plant an orange seed and expect to grow an apple tree; it is just impossible.

Education

This is a very important factor. When you educate yourself in areas you want to be good at, you become confident. I have come across people in a working environment and even in daily life activities; they like to lead but, unfortunately, they get nervous when it comes to leading people or a group, simply because they lack self-belief and confidence. This usually happens because they have no knowledge of what it takes to lead, or to be a leader etc. They also lack self-belief.

Successful people educate themselves in areas they are pursuing. For example, if you want to be a real estate investor, the best thing to do is to learn all you need to know in that field. By the time you have learnt all there is to know, this will enhance your self-belief and confidence and eventually you will become a master. The benefit of being confident in your area of work is that it will lead to more achievements simply because it will reflect in your attitude, self-image and, as a result, people will pick up on it.

Imagine you are at work and your boss runs into your office and screams in panic that there's a fire. How do you think you will react? You will panic even more than he did. As a leader you are expected to be bold, courageous, a problem solver and to stay calm in stressful situations. That's why you have followers as a leader, because they believe in you and also more importantly, they believe they can rely on you.

When a leader panics in front of his/her followers, this basically gives them reason to panic even more, due to the fact that they would feel that their security is gone. Successful people are usually leaders who motivate, set an example, inspire others to believe and follow suit. Why are successful people successful? This is simply because they do the little things unsuccessful people don't do, for example, they are willing to take risk, if the gain is right.

Association

Association is another important method widely used when trying to develop mental strength. People associate with one another for various reasons, for example learning, fun, teaching, sharing opinions pertaining to areas of interest, business, favours etc. All these are types of reasons why people associate with one another.

To get better at something, or even to achieve something, it is only common sense to associate with people who are good at what you are trying to get better at or achieve. Let's say, for instance, you want to get better at running. If you keep on running with people that aren't as good or as fast as you, you will never get better. To get better at something, whether it be sport or anything in particular, you simply have to associate yourself with the right kind of people, whom you can learn from, compete with, challenge etc. For example, if you want to be a better boxer, you will have to compete with a boxer who is better than you.

My mentor always used to say, "Dress for the job you want, not for the job you have." What he meant by this was simple. Imagine you are a junior manager in a company, seeking promotion to the senior management level. What you really ought to do is act like a senior manager, talk like a senior manager, take on the responsibilities of a senior manager if possible, surround yourself with senior managers etc. When you do this, you will start to learn a great deal from them.

Action

When trying to develop mental strength, this is as important as visualization. "It is good to dream, but it is good to dream and work." If you really study and observe successful people, especially in relation to how their career progressed, you will realize that once they make a decision pertaining to any project, they are quick to follow up with an action.

When you look around you, you will find out that we are surrounded by good dreamers who remain only dreamers. Why? They simply fail to act out their dream. We all have ideas, which bombard our minds; only most people do little or nothing about it because of disbelief, critical thinking, laziness, negative self-talk etc.

There is a common saying that I love, which is, "Everyone wants to go to heaven, but no one wants to die." This is very true when you think about it. People talk about if only I could be rich; if only I could get more time off work to start a part-time business; if only I could have more time to spend with my family, loved ones etc. We've all heard people say this consistently. If you are that type of person, one thing I want you to know is that you can. If only you commit to take the first step in faith, regardless of your previous and current situation. "Man is so made that when anything fires his soul, impossibilities vanish" (Jean de la Fontaine).

People fail to act because of fear: "What if it doesn't work, what will people say?" We usually behave this way due to the conditioning of our minds; we've managed to condition our minds so that we can only achieve so much, due to years of negative self-talk.

Complacency is another reason why people who dream of success fail to achieve it. I have come across people who will not change their jobs, even if they are to get a pay cut; they don't mind so long as they can hold on to their jobs. This might baffle you a little bit, but one thing that I have come to realize – even though strange it is true – is that such people suffer purely from self-limitation.

Emotional strength

In order to really understand how the power of self-belief can lead to success you will need to also understand how to develop emotional strength. So what is emotional strength? This is an ability to control an intense feeling, which might develop due to a particular event in our lives, for example, disappointments, anger, anxiety, etc.

When we are able to control our feelings, then we develop emotional strength. So many people lack emotional strength, which is one of the reasons they fail to achieve what their heart desires.

We all experience phases or stages in our lives that make us feel down or sad. If you are a person of purpose and of ambition, you need to develop emotional strength in other to see past all the obstacles you might face on your journey to achieve what you desire, that is, your goals.

The road to success, as any successful person will tell you, is rough and narrow. More importantly, it's an emotional roller coaster.

When you believe in yourself, you will be able to take the first step towards achieving your goals, because you will feel confident. But this is only the beginning. When you then develop emotional strength, it is more like a shield, which protects you from attacks. For example, if someone you work with irritates you. Your normal reaction would be to respond emotionally towards that person.

But when you can manage to control your temper, and instead talk things through with that person who offended you, giving a detailed explanation as to why you are offended, you will be controlling your emotions by doing so. I am sure you are beginning to understand how it works. For every obstacle we overcome on our journey to achieve success, we get strengthened, mentally and emotionally.

Spiritual Strength

As human beings we all have a limit, a breaking point when we feel, or say, enough is enough, I can't bear it any longer. Many people who work very hard towards achieving their goals give up at the very last minute, simply because things aren't happening as quickly as they would like them to be.

I am a strong believer in "What is worth doing at all is worth doing well", because I believe we should always finish what we started. We all know nothing comes easy, especially good things. Most of the time, when our victory is near, that's when it seems so far, and that's when we face the most negative situations.

With me personally, spiritual strength has helped me achieve most of my goals, through prayers and having unshakeable faith. So what is spiritual strength, exactly? Spiritual strength is an unshakeable feeling which strengthens us and helps us to see past, and overcome, our challenges in life, even when we are weak. Spiritual strength comes from above. A good example would be believing in a supreme being, God.

As a Christian, I have learnt to overcome my problems by seeing them as challenges, not problems. When you view your dilemmas as challenges instead of problems, it gives you reason and motivation to conquer them one by one, no matter how long it takes. To conquer is to overcome, rise above, win etc. Anytime I happen to face a challenge, what I usually do is pray to God before I act. The reason for this is that when I pray to God I feel so much alive, peaceful and confident about how to solve my situation, no matter how big or small the challenges might seem.

Spiritual strength is in the development of the human spirit or soul. When you develop spiritual strength it will enable you to think clearly and prevent you from worrying all the time, which leads to stress. By developing spiritual strength, whenever you face obstacles in your life you won't panic, but instead consult with and rely on the superpower that's responsible for the creation of the universe. Also by doing so, you will slowly but surely overcome your obstacles and end up being the success you deserve to be.

You Must Not Quit

"When things go wrong, as they sometime will,
when the road you are trudging seems all uphill,
when the funds are low and the debts are high,
and you want to smile, but you have to sigh,
rest if you must, but don't you quit.

Life is queer with its twist and turns,
as every one of us sometimes learns.
And many a fellow turns about when he might have won, had they stuck it out.
Don't give up though the pace seems slow,
you may succeed with another blow.

Success is failure turned inside out.
The silver tint of the clouds of doubts,
and you never can tell how close you are,
it may be near when it seems so far.
So stick to the fight when you are hardest hit,
it's when things seem worst that you must not quit".

(source unknown)

(Think)

If you think you are beaten, you are. If you think you dare not, you don't.
If you'd like to win but you think you can't, you can almost be certain you won't.
If you think that you'll lose, you are lost, for out in the world you will find success begins with a person's will; it's all in the state of the mind.
If you think you're outclassed you are; you've got to think high to rise.
You've just got to be sure of yourself before you can win the prize. Life battles don't always go to a stronger or faster man; but sooner or later the person who wins is the person that thinks they can.

(Anonymous)

Twenty years from now you will be more disappointed by the things you didn't do than by the ones you did do. So throw off the bowlines. Sail the safe harbor. Catch the trade winds in your sails. Explore. Dream.

(Mark Twain)

Consult not your fears but your hopes and your dreams. Think not of your frustrations, but about your unfulfilled potential. Concern yourself not with what you tried and failed in, but with what it is possible for you to do.

(source unknown)

In any moment of decision, the best thing you can do is the right thing, and the worst thing you can do is nothing.

(Theodore Roosevelt)

Many people dream of success, to me success can only be achieved through repeated failure and introspection.

(Soichiro Honda, founder of Honda)

People become really quite remarkable when they start thinking that they can do things. When they believe in themselves they have the first secret of success.

(Norman Vincent Peale)

Take the first step in faith. You don't have to see the whole staircase, take the first step.

(Dr Martin Luther King Jr)

The "Strangest Secret" by Earl Nightingale

Some years ago, the late Nobel prize-winning Dr. Albert Schweitzer was asked by a reporter, "Doctor, what's wrong with men today?" The great doctor was silent a moment, and then he said, "Men simply don't think!"

It's about this that I want to talk with you. We live today in a golden age. This is an era that humanity has looked forward to, dreamed of, and worked toward for thousands of years. We live in the richest era that ever existed on the face of the earth ... a land of abundant opportunity for everyone.

However, if you take 100 individuals who start even at the age of 25, do you have any idea what will happen to those men and women by the time they're 65? These 100 people believe they're going to be successful. They are eager toward life, there is a certain sparkle in their eye, an erectness to their carriage, and life seems like a pretty interesting adventure to them.

But by the time they're 65, only one will be rich, four will be financially independent, five will still be working, and 54 will be broke — depending on others for life's necessities.

Only five out of 100 make the grade! Why do so many fail? What has happened to the sparkle that was there when they were 25? What has become of the dreams, the hopes, the plans ... and why is there such a large disparity between what these people intended to do and what they actually accomplished.

THE DEFINITION OF SUCCESS

First, we have to define success and here is the best definition I've ever been able to find: "Success is the progressive realization of a worthy ideal."

A success is the school teacher who is teaching because that's what he or she wanted to do. A success is the entrepreneur who starts his own company because that was his dream - that's what he wanted to do. A success is the salesperson who wants to become the best salesperson in his or her company and sets forth on the pursuit of that goal.

A success is anyone who is realizing a worthy predetermined ideal, because that's what he or she decided to do ... deliberately. But only one out of 20 does that! The rest are "failures."

Rollo May, the distinguished psychiatrist, wrote a wonderful book called Man's Search for Himself, and in this book he says: "The opposite of courage in our society is not cowardice ... it is conformity." And there you have the reason for so many failures. Conformity — people acting like everyone else, without knowing why or where they are going.

We learn to read by the time we're seven. We learn to make a living by the time we're 30. Often by that time we're not only making a living, we're supporting a family. And yet by the time we're 65, we haven't learned how to become financially independent in the richest land that has ever been known. Why? We conform! Most of us are acting like the wrong percentage group — the 95 who don't succeed.

GOALS

Have you ever wondered why so many people work so hard and honestly without ever achieving anything in particular, and why others don't seem to work hard, yet seem to get everything? They seem to have the "magic touch." You've heard people say, "Everything he touches turns to gold." Have you ever noticed that a person who becomes successful tends to continue to become more successful? And, on the other hand, have you noticed how someone who's a failure tends to continue to fail

The difference is goals. People with goals succeed because they know where they're going. It's that simple. Failures, on the other hand, believe that their lives are shaped by circumstances ... by things that happen to them ... by exterior forces.

Think of a ship with the complete voyage mapped out and planned. The captain and crew know exactly where the ship is going and how long it will take — it has a definite goal. And 9,999 times out of 10,000, it will get there.

Now let's take another ship — just like the first — only let's not put a crew on it, or a captain at the helm. Let's give it no aiming point, no goal, and no destination. We just start the engines and let it go. I think you'll agree that if it gets out of the harbor at all, it will either sink or wind up on some deserted beach — a derelict. It can't go anyplace because it has no destination and no guidance.

It's the same with a human being. However, the human race is fixed, not to prevent the strong from winning, but to prevent the weak from losing. Society today can be likened to a convoy in time of war. The entire society is slowed down to protect its weakest link, just as the naval convoy has to go at the speed that will permit its slowest vessel to remain in formation.

That's why it's so easy to make a living today. It takes no particular brains or talent to make a living and support a family today. We have a plateau of so-called "security." So, to succeed, all we must do is decide how high above this plateau we want to aim.

Throughout history, the great wise men and teachers, philosophers, and prophets have disagreed with one another on many different things. It is only on this one point that they are in complete and unanimous agreement — the key to success and the key to failure is this:

WE BECOME WHAT WE
THINK ABOUT

This is The Strangest Secret! Now, why do I say it's strange, and why do I call it a secret? Actually, it isn't a secret at all. It was first promulgated by some of the earliest wise men, and it appears again and again throughout the Bible. But very few people have learned it or understand it. That's why it's strange, and why for some equally strange reason it virtually remains a secret.

Marcus Aurelius, the great Roman Emperor, said: "A man's life is what his thoughts make of it."

Disraeli said this: "Everything comes if a man will only wait ... a human being with a settled purpose must accomplish it, and nothing can resist a will that will stake even existence for its fulfillment."

William James said: "We need only in cold blood act as if the thing in question were real, and it will become infallibly real by growing into such a connection with our life that it will become real. It will become so knit with habit and emotion that our interests in it will be those which characterize belief." He continues, " ... only you must, then, really wish these things, and wish them exclusively, and not wish at the same time a hundred other incompatible things just as strongly."

My old friend Dr. Norman Vincent Peale put it this way: "If you think in negative terms, you will get negative results. If you think in positive terms, you will achieve positive results."

George Bernard Shaw said: "People are always blaming their circumstances for what they are. I don't believe in circumstances. The people who get on in this world are the people who get up and look for the circumstances they want, and if they can't find them, make them."

Well, it's pretty apparent, isn't it?

We become what we think about. A person who is thinking about a concrete and worthwhile goal is going to reach it, because that's what he's thinking about. Conversely, the person who has no goal, who doesn't know where he's going, and whose thoughts must therefore be thoughts of confusion, anxiety, fear, and worry will thereby create a life of frustration, fear, anxiety and worry. And if he thinks about nothing ... he becomes nothing.

AS YE SOW - SO SHALL YE REAP

The human mind is much like a farmer's land. The land gives the farmer a choice.

He may plant in that land whatever he chooses. The land doesn't care what is planted. It's up to the farmer to make the decision. The mind, like the land, will return what stances ... people to lives of suc you plant, but it doesn't care what you plant. If the farmer plants two seeds - one a seed of corn, the other nightshade, a deadly poison, waters and takes care of the land, what will happen

Remember, the land doesn't care. It will return poison in just as wonderful abundance as it will corn. So up come the two plants - one corn, one poison as it's written in the Bible, "As ye sow, so shall ye reap."

The human mind is far more fertile, far more incredible and mysterious than the land, but it works the same way. It doesn't care what we plant ... success ... or failure. A concrete, worthwhile goal ... or confusion, misunderstanding, fear, anxiety, and so on. But what we plant it must return to us.

The problem is that our mind comes as standard equipment at birth. It's free. And things that are given to us for nothing, we place little value on. Things that we pay money for, we value.

The paradox is that exactly the reverse is true. Everything that's really worthwhile in life came to us free - our minds, our souls, our bodies, our hopes, our dreams, our ambitions, our intelligence, our love of family and children and friends and country. All these priceless possessions are free.

But the things that cost us money are actually very cheap and can be replaced at any time. A good man can be completely wiped out and make another fortune. He can do that several times. Even if our home burns down, we can rebuild it. But the things we got for nothing, we can never replace. Our mind can do any kind of job we assign to it, but generally speaking, we use it for little jobs instead of big ones. So decide now. What is it you want? Plant your goal in your mind. It's the most important decision you'll ever make in your entire life.

Do you want to excel at your particular job? Do you want to go places in your company ... in your community? Do you want to get rich? All you have got to do is plant that seed in your mind, care for it, work steadily toward your goal, and it will become a reality.

It not only will, there's no way that it cannot. You see, that's a law — like the laws of Sir Isaac Newton, the laws of gravity. If you get on top of a building and jump off, you'll always go down — you'll never go up.

And it's the same with all the other laws of nature. They always work. They're inflexible. Think about your goal in a relaxed, positive way. Picture yourself in your mind's eye as having already achieved this goal. See yourself doing the things you will be doing when you have reached your goal.

Every one of us is the sum total of our own thoughts. We are where we are because that's exactly where we really want or feel we deserve to be — whether we'll admit that or not. Each of us must live off the fruit of our thoughts in the future, because what you think today and tomorrow — next month and next year — will mold your life and determine your future. You're guided by your mind.

I remember one time I was driving through eastern Arizona and I saw one of those giant earth-moving machines - roaring along the road with what looked like 30 tons of dirt in it - a tremendous, incredible machine - and there was a little man perched way up on top with the wheel in his hands, guiding it. As I drove along I was struck by the similarity of that machine to the human mind. Just suppose you're sitting at the controls of such a vast source of energy. Are you going to sit back and fold your arms and let it run itself into a ditch? Or are you going to keep both hands firmly on the wheel and control and direct this power to a specific, worthwhile purpose? It's up to you. You're in the driver's seat.

You see, the very law that gives us success is a double-edged sword. We must control our thinking. The same rule that can lead people to lives of success, wealth, happiness, and all the things they ever dreamed of — that very same law can lead them into the gutter. It's all in how they use it … for good or for bad. That is The Strangest Secret!

I once read about a man named Grove Patterson who was the editor in chief of the *Toledo Daily Blade*. He made a speech which concluded like this:

"My years in the newspaper business have convinced me of several things, among them that people are basically good and that we came from someplace and we're going someplace. So we should take care to make our time here an exciting adventure. The architect of the universe didn't build a stairway leading nowhere and the greatest teacher of all - the carpenter from the plains of galilee gave us the secret time and time again.

"As ye believe so shall it be done unto you".

Do what the experts since the dawn of recorded history have told us to do: pay the price, by becoming the person you want to become. It's not nearly as difficult as living unsuccessfully.

The moment you decide on a goal to work toward, you're immediately a successful person — you are then in that rare group of people who know where they're going. Out of every hundred people, you belong to the top five. Don't concern yourself too much with how you are going to achieve your goal — leave that completely to a power greater than yourself. All you have to do is know where you're going. The answers will come to you of their own accord, and at the right time.

Start today. You have nothing to lose — but you have your whole life to win.

My Final Thoughts and Dedication

I believe this book will be of great help to you, the reader, which is the main reason why I wrote it, so I can share my knowledge and experience with anyone who reads it.

I also wrote it to inform you the reader, that you can achieve anything you want in life, so long as you believe in yourself and take the necessary action towards achieving your goals in life.

Always stay focused, regardless of your situation; there will always be a better day.

I dedicate this book to God, for giving me the inspiration to write and knowledge to share. I also dedicate this book to my mentors, friends and family.